Gregory Gunn

ALSO AVAILABLE BY THE AUTHOR:

POETRY

EARTHLY AND ETHEREAL ENCOUNTERS, 1995

REGARDING OBLIVION, 2005

http://www.geocities.com/jkandromeda/gregorywilliamgunn.html

The Rest is Silence

Gregory Wm. Gunn

authorHOUSE®

AuthorHouse™
1663 Liberty Drive, Suite 200
Bloomington, IN 47403
www.authorhouse.com
Phone: 1-800-839-8640

First published by AuthorHouse 2/18/2008

ISBN: 978-1-4343-5476-1 (sc)

Printed in the United States of America
Bloomington, Indiana

This book is printed on acid-free paper.

Dedication:

For those who never seem to receive favourable winds, halcyon seas or a clear view of the nightsky to assist in their navigation homeward.

Acknowledgements

Some of these poems or portions thereof have previously appeared in the following periodicals:

The poem TANGENCY as it appears herein was previously published by INKKO PUBLISHING: INSCRIBED MAGAZINE.

Notes in the Cosmic Fugue, Penny Dreadful and Pendragon Publications, One Earth, and Cosmic Trend.

Author photo: J.C. Chertoff

A special appreciation to Andreas Gripp for his editorial erudition regarding the early edition of this collection. The final product would not have been as concise and precise without his astute eye for detail.

Table of Contents

BRIGHT STAR

Bright star, would I were steadfast as thou art---
   Not in lone spendour hung aloft the night
And watching, with eternal lids apart,
   Like nature's patient, sleepless Eremite,
The moving waters at their priestlike task
   Of pure ablution round earth's human shores,
Or gazing on the new soft fallen mask
   Of snow upon the mountains and the moors---
No---yet still steadfast, still unchangeable,
   Pillow'd upon my fair love's ripening breast,
To feel for ever its soft fall and swell,
   Awake for ever in a sweet unrest,
Still, still to hear her tender-taken breath,
   And so live ever---or else swoon to death.

---John Keats, 1795 - 1821

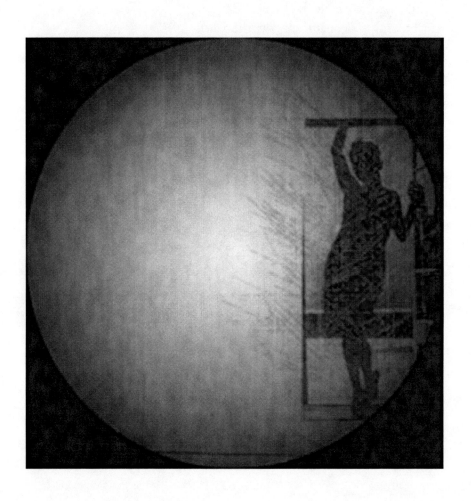

THRESHOLD

A diminutive brittle girl
lay rigid as ice on our stoop.
We stumbled upon her
one starless night
on Winter's threshold,
breast down in the snow
like a silenced junco nestling
crushed by unforgiving frost.

Ever since her arrival,
we dare not risk stepping
over that ominous doorsill,
her young body clad
in meringue blouse
and soufleéd skirt
exuding a curious lactic,
fluent opaqueness.

Now we must constrain
ourselves as we dwell
within this fairy-tale safehouse,
light as eiderdown,
cleaning systematically,
keeping all in fine fettle,
sweeping away tedium,
allowing our actions
& reactions to shuttlecock
between us, attached
to imperceptible lines,
dispositions given
complete carte blanche.

Flagrant orders of the day
remain of no account,
frothy and stagnant,
they grant no soulless riders
to gallop through
the silvered backside
of this lucid looking glass
where a likeness
of this sister of ours
is imbued in splintered
Alice blue moonbeams,
and all the while
her heady aroma
distends and ascends
across another threshold.

THE UNFALLEN STATE

Each dawn the insentient sea begins
anew, numb to the fact that it
is the Mediterranean, so it sleeps in,
oblivious to society's waters of bitterness;
politically neutral concerning colours
such as traditional Capri blue.
The great sea stops her ears
and shuts her eyes to History's
drowned sailors.

The names Poseidon, Jonah & Caesar
mean nothing to her. Each dawn
is a tabula rasa, for she has no memories,
& like infancy, every moment
is wondrous & adventuresome.
We watch the tiny ones with awe
& smile for they haven't discovered
any meaning behind nor display
any of their colours.

MYTHOS

Transfixed as these gilded laurels,
I'm spreading strong roots similar
to a Gordian knot along this alcove
as Aurora's maiden light dispels
a saffron mist & cannot otherwise
be composed & unshielded:
a coppice virtuous as Artemis.

Why then should such an image
as this ever unsettle my psyche;
drenching reason with purposeless
self-reproach as though those leaves
were to be the cascading curls
of an alluring Daphne trying
to deceive the Apollo within me?

MONARCH OF MAY

What lures the ocean breeze this distance
inland? It is the redolence of magnolia
that annuls the summers ago amid
this border and that breakoff point,
tantalising the nostrils, tearing the eyes,
contrasting me with you & vice versa.

Girl who garlanded a crown of blooms,
then coronated me, might I have uttered
a caveat before becoming your Monarch
of May by your design? Should I have
exempted you from all that suffering
& not subjected you to disillusionment--
you who were once imperial & jovial?

TANGENCY

I retract
the ruler-straight,
acute angles of anger,
unbending degrees of unruliness,
the gradation of frustration
miscalculated.

Even a semester
of prosperity's protraction
never factored
into the equation.

The unlearnt capacity
of end points, intangible
unknown variables
resulted in disorientation:
a small-scale roundabout morning
while the abstruse principal
chalks the next problem.

My shaping imagination
wanders from the subject,
I become a second satellite,
falling at right angles
to the earth,
cutting a sun-splashed figure,
my circumference
beyond the clouded
rational horizon.

I decline
geometric formulae
and theorems, profess
that when the final cycle
is terminated,
I'll be an immaculate arc of acuity
on a galactic plane
at eye level with a higher
class of star clusters.

LAKE SIMCOE ESSENTIAL

Picture Northern Ontario's
cottage country in all its intrinsic,
mystic resplendence.

Visualise wine purple raspberries
and apple green pears
in late Summer, sallow starlit
shafts penetrating
the primrose adjacent
shore's sunset afterglow.

Bring to mind the prevalent,
piquant scent of spruce, pine---
an evocation of evergreens
instilled with weeping stones
the Merlin magic of moonlight
on Wedgwood blue water.

So summon up the morning,
your skeleton
stirring in spreading tendrils
of aureate sunshine,
your cheeks
warm with a mantle
of Fall's first frost.

This is the natural world's
arcanum, an unquelled
matin of physicality,
the prized provisions we
stockpile for the dead
of Winter.

SOLSTICE

Nearly gone
the vesper hours'
cantaloupe sunlight
is minimal,
and accompanying
her fading is your final
thoughtful gaze;
one last chance
for clarity to decode
the scattering of stellar
out-of-mind matters
with which
you identifly.

Superb contrast
of inseparableness
though your face
is stardusted,
you still care
about the forthcoming
Winter's refracted
contours. Love's
isostatic tendencies
sustain our heart's
Sun at perigee,
prominent in proper
season on its
own meridian.

COLD AIR MASSES

Your requiem is rising
from a wailing sea. It blends
among inconsolable gull cries,
beyond your hearing.

Every fluctuating wave
calls to mind your unexpectant
departure, and now there is
no unharboured bird more
destitute than I.

Your requiem is rising
from a wailing sea,
about to abort your awayness
& skepticism with yet more
in the series of I-love-you's.

I would make an effort
to summon my sea-bird back
from sunless soaring heights
for your requiem is still rising
from a wailing sea.

ICY ABSTRACTION

We have swept & ranged
over a region of high-reaching hills
to arrive in an uncharted territory
where sky is frost-checkered
crystal scaled into a Moiré effect.
December stacks up
on window sills;
in our hearts the winter widens.
We are indeed in new environs
and alienated.

If you were to expire here,
being brittle;
to die after only one cold season,
and the inverted year
were to evacuate the hilltops
eventually, would not the snowdrifts
dissolve in our hearts,
the river wash away the winter,
and I then to inhabit
untested grounds standing alone
in the sunlight?

The North wind tells me
that in this new land
the winter lingers
a long time, nearly
to the extent
of a Springtide Oblivion.

SNOWSCAPE

iridescent flakes invigorate
our weary visions,
we drift to a pristine woodland:
chaste, impressionless,
unvisited trails,
air smelling of prosperity,
keeping vigil over us.

the snow stirs us on,
lily-white caparisoned
steeplechasers gallop
through an argent archway
of firs, beside
a ghostly lake
where the last spite
of sun softens
a milky-misted aura
round the rising moon.

like crested childhood
memories, falling crystals crown us--
full dreams ahead,
the lustre instigates
its white magic
on shiftless February fields.

puffed out feathers
penetrate the scarlet eye
of the solitary
snowbird:
our hearts, flashing flames
under sheer veneers,
hedonistic blood races
on full cry
along the glittering trail
leading us into the night.

REPEAT EPISODES

Nine long months have passed
since you've returned to this home,
back for just the short term.

Pieces of you are starting
to fill places out of vacuum's
reach;
settling into dust formations,
resembling several versions
of the amalgamated one I loved:
a relaxed-arms-behind-the-head-you,
a standing-defiantly-akimbo-you,
a throw-caution-to-the-wind-you.

That black, sexy silk chemise
hanging in my bedroom closet
still retains your figure:
it might even strut on its own
through the front door, avoiding
my vague grabbing attempts to
thwart its advancement.

You had to demonstrate self-
sufficiency, *find my free-spirit space,*
you said. Gone away to focus on
artistic endeavours, somewhere
that might as well have been
in the upper atmosphere,
far from my vantage point
while I stared blankly each day
at a blur of grey madness.

This house never seemed so huge.
All your false airs
shadowed your escape route
like a slick, 40's flick gumshoe,
yet I can't find time enough
to write all the words accumulating
in my mind, images crashing
into one another;
intermingling metaphors
like wave after wave of bad tidings
breaking the strand in threes.

Soon you'll get the urge to break
away again, and with each episode,
the gap grows wider as though we stand
apart on divided sides
of an overflowing river,
resorting to smoke signals & semaphore
to communicate, slipping into separate
lives like the red cotton sheets
I left outside in the overnight rain,
then dried in the morning sun,
shrunken so they won't fit
the bed
anymore.

CLEARING

I had wandered
from the grip of aggravation,
looking for refuge
in a forest of forbearance.

No cell, blackberry
nor iPod, no ties
to technology whatsoever,
    disconnected
beneath these branches,
only a scolding blue jay
might deliver
a dissonant dispatch.

Fists to unclench,
shoulders to untighten,
seeking absolution
from self-inflicted guilt.
Regret *in absentia*
as serene thoughts
are garnered,
idyllic ideas form.

How can I not envy,
and learn lessons
from these woodland
denizens' uncomplicated ways:
grey squirrel's scurrying,
jack rabbit's nonchalance,
tamarack's true upward growth,
the sparrow's song
with no spitefulness?

Below my skin lies
the simple understanding
of a mourning dove's
plaintive coo,
and the trees' sturdiness.

Recovering equipoise,
I forage oriels within,
hiking onward for an
objective that might
clear my conscience
of every last stain of blame.

MALAISE

Through long lashes
your stinging stare
has scattered trepidation
deep below my skin.
The rumour-montage
of lying lips breaches
every promise,
stockades my lust.

O tormentor
of corpuscles,
every bodily gesture
ashames me to ashes,
causes my body
to tremble and buckle.
The scent of your
hair & bosom
burns my eyes.

Why drag me out,
stripped naked
into the scorching sun
for all the world
to see the severity
of such wounds?

Accede to the pipe's
announcing the final
act, since I shall
never pursue
the harlequin's tune
involuntarily anymore.

That type of show
mustn't go on,
so behind the veil
of your lips, unsheathe
your rapierlike tongue,
and in my humility
plunge it to the hilt.

DIM-SIGHTED LOVE

For years on end we contained
all happier, earlier days in total
diplomatic immunity,
in the cellar, provided them
every liberty, ungoverned
by time and reset into motion
like vaulted ambitions, yet
they paraded through every room,
each facade reproduced in reflections,
wearing themselves to shadows,
fading from sight between
the drawing room & vestibule
as amber amazement blasted
through the front door.

March moved in, peppered
with bitterness, a patriarchal
image accepted defeat & laid
down to weep,
recounted reminders
from that purple period
of excessive blue premises
where our hearts were
snapped & crushed like peanut shells
by our own hands & undoing,
for we hungered for higher quality
delights, purer gourmand fare.
O dim-sighted Love!

INVENTORY

The time to take stock
of my psyche is overdue,
flipping through ledgers
for vital interests
that weren't itemised
equitably in the past.

My overtaxed heart
weighs heavily
in the balance,
as exemption
may be but one
outstanding debt.

I shall examine
thoroughly storerooms
of hurt, constantly
tripping over cartons
of loneliness,

begging you to join
me to pore over
these dimly-lit spaces.
There's a source
of forgiveness
in here somewhere:

a waterfall to wash
my tartan temper;
liquidate all my
unaccountabilities,
purge the pain
and slake our thirsts.

SHADOW MAN

I am shadow man
with exquisite bones.

I minister to them
with vigilance, as well as
an out of the pale blue
kind of pathos.

They are shone monthly
like precious metals.

Bloodstones & bachelor
buttons are presently
not in season.

One day, when fortitude
is regained, I'll carry off
the object of my affections
and establish
a resplendent reliquary
in her honour.

In lieu of my lover's truant
heart, I shall dangle
like a pentangular pendant.

Emptiness recently replete,
who is this clearheaded
spectator in you?

You wander about,
you move with moxie;
your every comportment
smites cloistered death
with consternation.

I accept your trepidation
like a peace offering.
Occasionally, when
settled in your bosom,
half-peeled lids open
fully and peer
through fluid eyes.

Then like chlorotic creeks,
childish, unexplored
dreams get underway
and begin to surge.

EQUILIBRIUM

I

Pass the farmer's market,
the trust company and the pharmacy,
beyond all obligatory points
on the way to the river;
and in the elapsing afternoon
the opal sky splits apart
like a massive sheet of ice,
dividing into lambent light
to exhibit in high relief
cerulean islands
in fields of daisy faces
gazing downward
on these vacant streets.

II

No phantoms frequent
here today
to plague my peace of mind,
this *esprit de corps*,
coalition of molecules.

Intersected in the instant,
my mass propels counter
to the earth
which queues everything
in alignment,
maintains the rhythm
toward its axis
in pursuit of perfection.

THE ROSE

THE ROSE OF JERICHO

When the heart is wayworn,
just can't supply an inspired word,
drifting onward to some foreign ambit.

At such time the once-adored
woman's hand ceases to clasp,
changes spent currency without weight
or worth in her lover's palms.

When our feet blaze few fresh paths
on parched, daisy-chained shores
with their blistering means.
When the sightless anatomy falls
to fragments under hollowness
as a spring draws back to delve
for its sunkened speech.

When shadows of approaching
arguments are cast in the hallway
where the grandfather clock runs amok.

When love loses it edge,
its pointedness erodes, and the reign
of St. Swithin commences over
this house letting the rose
of Jericho manifest at our gateway
with cardinal emblems, nobleman
and a vassal
in flamboyant vestments.

Then allow the winds
to be expectant as a wild prophet;
permit the anima
into our heart-of-hearts:
blood blossom,
white dove of discord,
sour petals, and an earthly
decree with a palatable sea wrack.

So sheathe your blade, and *you*,
draw up your gowns like bundles
of sails decked out, fore-and-aft.
Make a spinnaker run
upon a glossy ocean,
a baptism of brine
in the leeward tidal current.

SOMERSET MEMORIAL

O what bleakness
that even a heavy sky's
hollow shapes creeping
over grey granite
cause a commotion,

under a tangerine sun,
tributaries counterflux
struck dumb by
the torrid heat.

A trinity of hickories
by the roadstead,
anticipating the Spring's
swelling braided brook.

On the churchyard's
knoll, an engraved
pyramid beneath
the low green tent:
the last home for
gone-to-glory soldiers.

What may they assimilate
from this nothingness
save for the stony sleep
into a senescent night?

COMPOSITION OF MORTAL FEAR

Like hooded January men
in woolen underwear,
we lumber snug
vested in our dermae.
Confronting the hunting grounds
in the open air.
We demonstrate *cervus civilis*
that designate demarcation.

And just as wildlife
we mark our territory
by urinating on bushes;
tagging the environs in our societal cells
with outdoor jacuzzis,
extravagant garden topiaries,
spoilt children, and manicured lawns.

From the other side
of the heather hedgerow,
skirting the two-car, interlocked laneway,
another bestial scent
trespasses.
Boundaries shudder with resentment,
a hint of blood.
We flourish solely
in the confines of our own aroma.
Frivolities thrive like ivy,
the peach tree blossoms, but her leaves
curl up and wither.

We exchange a live macaw
for one fast-dyed feather,
obstruct the moonlight
for pulsating city neon signs,
the entire *Global Village*
for me   lonely & petrified.

YIELD

In this wearisome way,
the ceaseless disagreements
continue. O how they it would
rollick in persuading me,
this provincialism with its
incontrovertible raven black
reasoning, its bile green
Parthian shots.

I am past its acid yellow
astringent assertions.
Forget all Machiavellian
subterfuge for I've lain supine,
assuming the complexion
of the wizened steppes;
the uneven, unrefined
rationale of unclipped barley.

My uncertain hand lets go
of its iron grip
on irrevocable bygone days
and weatherworn,
chain-link fence.

I yield in succession
each fuzzy peach
that had clung,
held fast like these obligations.
Present day objectives
percolate from my pores.
My vision drifts amid
vast abstracts
of independant skies.

Focussing on those
clingstones and sighing.
It's merely a matter of minutes
when I shall inherit
their inference.

For goodness sake
no disturbances please!

ACCOMPLISHMENT

We long to have it all:
    to expand & absorb,
    to compress & extract,
to designate that space
where out of the sphere of us
creation carries on
ferocious as a hungry wolf.

We want the brutal growling stomach,
the burden of proof in the stirring blood
exciting the hide and snarling
the frame into action.

We demand magnified vision
to see the finite & infinite,
the near & the far.

We yearn to have our language
sirenic with madrigals
to arouse even the Draconian
among us.

We hope for the endowment
to measure up to the hands
of the Supreme Being,
to shape with our fingers,
caressing clay into artistic merit---

We aspire to feel accomplishment.

A DIFFERENT SENSE

In the afterglow
of a central eclipse,
his fingertips give attention
to the world's
embossed communiqués,
a syncopated white stick
beats out his anguish,
cravings, the meter
of his respiration.

Colours consisting
of both matter and energy,
precipitating and streaming
an inflection:
a silver, textured sonata
arranged on his black
eyelid music sheets.

He has a special sensitivity
to the floral scents,
perhaps is the only poet
who is captivated
by their mosaic melodies.

APPREHENSION

Call not on me tonight,
pose no further questions
for I am unanswerable
and pensive.

Demand nothing now,
my dearest, as dusk
descends.

Please pardon me
if at odd times
my interest shifts
elsewhere;
to restless winds stirring
from the world's other side,
spinning sly ciphers.

My trembling spirit
breathes uneasily,
swirling in sidereal darkness.

Do not worry if I seem
distant, turning a deaf ear
to you and instead
heed as a lying wolf might,
a distinctive sound
or scent from a slinking
forest dweller.

Quickly disquietude
may fade into a dream
where your delicate eyes
appear as blue
forget-me-nots
inevitably bewildered.

TRAPEZE DAYS

Curled maple leaves perform
cartwheels across bedraggled grass
in April's rolling wind, and my thoughts
immediately turn to our trapeze days:
all our unnecessary danglings in order
to entertain on-lookers. The tension
between you and me became tight
as a highwire, led to iodine calamities.
Was it the ups and downs or rather
misjugglery that I took an unnetted
tumble from your good graces?

APRIL'S ARRIVAL

The radiant dayglow marches
upon the white dust long since
settled, sullied & spoilt.
Snowlines expose their arteries
and Earth's heart unstrings
      amid hustling headstreams.

The Winter capsizes,
breaches like a birch canoe's
hull, Mother Nature lies naked
beneath jaundiced lichens,
miniature mudslides.
Newspaper scraps & memories
turn into a black & white
      trickle in tiny creeks.

Gold & purple crocuses
peek from underneath
spreading junipers
as Spring blazes upon leprous
concrete, undertaking
the illustrious panache
of pagan divinities, marred
      but crowned with success.

MAKING AN ALP OUT OF AN ANTHILL

Significant insects seemingly inch
importantly along the flagstones,
scrambling up shoots of snap peas,
circumspecting all the land
with uninquisitive yet complex eyes,
and come to realise the earth is far
too complicated: these greater lengths
beyond their limited scope
of comprehension, so they stagger
back down to solid ground to stake
claim on diverse districts in vain.

Other narcissistic bugs arrogantly
adopt motley motifs and fine lustres
in order to attract attention;
a sexual signalling, and still others,
with no ulterior motives, choose patchy
camouflage just intending to somehow
blend in. The majority have no language
per se, except for a feeble, instinctive
chatter of non-stop ineptitude.

Gather courage, my friends:
entomologists are in error who report
factors of a human nature observed
in these invasive insects' methods,
irrespective of their industrious,
intricate interchange. After all,
significant insects aren't really social
climbers, they merely appear to be.

BREAKTHROUGH

Irrespective of futile knees
genuflecting & unavailing
pressed palms raised in praise
to self-absorbed deities
in a monolithic Shrangri-la,
despite the system of belief
that has sunk into shambles,
the sanguine cocoon breaks open,
and the caterpillar
gains its freedom.

For always the impelling
ballet of nature is omnipresent,
its perpetual pirouetting
within a stirring cervix
of wind; an ecstatic daybreak
following the infirmity
of total darkness.

THE CHANGELING

You sense your libido receding,
your skin losing sensitivity to touch.

You are metamorphosing
into a nonseminal & asexual entity.

The empress in the inky sky,
draped in purloined raiments
of mother-of-pearl is encircled
by a tenuous harlequin band.

You hang in doubt about her stability,
her cool otherworldly equilibrium.

You feel the need to eclipse the moon,
to convolve through the streets
like a glowworm dispersing omni-
directional radiance in the blackness.

The objective:

> to writhe with luminous energy,
> prevail here on the earth, shadowless,
> crystalline, impelling constantly
> onward.

DISCOVERY

Sludge, aquatic plant life,
soft blowing wind profuse
with swelter & rhizome aromas;
and to the extreme north
the creeping shelf ice.

Melting and freezing points
unite efforts on earth,
the planet a tangible ambiguity,
expressly supposable
like water on the sun's surface.

At this stage,
in the landmark of discovery,
yours is a frenetic orderliness,
a prelude to the promenade
of parts in the offing,
of limbs still latent.

You are an enterprising
salamander self-assured,
balanced on the edge
of two worlds, emerged
from the river, about to test
solid ground.

STREAMING DISTRESS

The rushing stream
has recovered
the atolls that I once
treasured, the keys
of composure are slowly
sinking away.

The oleander is less
lovely and ambrosial
than we first had taken
at face value.

The rising water
has merely a sprinkling
of mysteries it
opens its mouth
to divulge.

This burdensome heart
plumbs the depths;
collapses under
the crux of high-
pressured sorrow.

Much too late
a timely intervening
sandbar or availing
shoal that might
have saved it.

THE SIREN OF BLITHE SOUND

Making my mouth water like a fine wine,
as palatable as a flawless al fresco painting,
you come to me like a welcome woman
I've imagined as the complete personification
of quixotism, unfadingly convinced of verses
long before I even blot up to compose them.

The fluidity of your midriff engenders music
belonging to us, our song a silver serpent
resolutely thrusting into discomfiture,
Sustaining savoury notes in the wistfulness
of long golden locks unravelled, releasing
the fragrance of the seaport at sunset.

Sing *a cappella*, my cantatrice, whenever
the harbour breezes command you, take
possession of your voice, sing jubilantly
to verify breath as your own innovation,
wail away blushed with soft crimson mist
to this bluff on the brow of a flushed Dawn.

ICARIAN DELUSIONS OF GRANDEUR

On this occasion
there won't be detachment,
no deviation from
paralysing stillness.

Unwavering skyward
on the precipice,
forehead keen
with the tranquillity
of the quest,
he's wholly aware
his viscera's aching void
might only be surfeited
by the flames in his veins.

Arms outstretched
buoyed with anticipation,
flight of fancy,
fire and fury
fused into one,
a pyric javelin
fallen humanity
heaved at Helios.

OCEANSIDE OBSERVATIONS

Like cherubic sole indentations in
the pale sands of the Promised Land,
scallops & starfish inlay the strand.
Gracefully gliding above your carnation
cottages, strident with niveous wings,
herons dive & make dead-stick landings
on the ochre loam of the bluff behind
an inverted, blue broken-hulled rowboat.

Above your ethereal world, airier still,
sideslips the raven-winged messenger
of death. You turn from sad news of today,
look out to sea to see whitecapped waves
appearing as teeth in a giant sardonic grin.
Countless backsliding invertebrates chase
small-scale glimmering goals. Life ad libs
a diverse array on this two-sided school
of thought, the unsound & the merciless.

CONTINUUM

Resurrection remains night's
sequel to blackness,
of dying past day's wisdom,
and yet we suppose it long
before we are ever sightless.

We're as perishable
as bonfire leaves aflame,
spiring heavenward, extinguished
shortly thereafter & grounded;
ashes once again consumed
by the earth that sprang us,
whose autumnal fires enlightened
a submissive man's mission,
burnt out on the other
side of recovery:

how might this lightlessness
of non-existence re-energise?

Inclemency of Winter's white
cannot conceive of Spring's
rebellious vibrancy until
the very moment makes it
clear, and we bear witness
to April's eye-filling aesthetics.

Revitalised, eternity rising up
through the soft soil
where tears of mourning
were wept for us, from out
the coldest, dusty night,
a most beautiful blossoming.

RESURFACING

Rays of hope & foreshadows
light under my ceiling, coupling
in robust accordance.
Learn of these odd wedded
rituals, my very close friend.

You flee from gathering clouds
and in your hands you trace
cardinal virtues.

Your voice is vigorous,
clear and articulate, faint
undertones follow you, so
pay attention, they are my
black veins serenading
in the moonless nightsky.

I am nameless and have no
characteristic complexion;
pleasant point of rendezvous
and dark room, paths
for dreams and rookery.

Oh, what a trenchant bed
of livid leaves the romance
gods have accommodated
for my lying next to you.

A dark horse gallops
on the misty coastline. I can
hear its hooves in subterranean
caves striking the wellspring
of my blood at its very acute
axis with the ebb of life.

Oh what a harvest time!
Whosoever could have had
such charm to transfer me
to this luscious, meandering
maidenhair, below the sands,
delicately blended with the salty
scent of driftwood;

from among the colourless
ages, fruition and desolation,
plus these rectrospections?
Receive this latent, open heart
of earth, everything pleasurable
in the darkness unconditionally
released & presented to you,
my trusted confidante.

The next morning and I had
resurfaced, stretching for
the warmth & bright light
of the sun, by noon my face
had bloomed; so come
to recognise your own splendid,
witnessed guidance;
an entire enigma harnessed
in your auspicious hands,
my most cherished love.

CELESTIAL ATTRACTION

It is abundantly clear,
the focal point from here
is nothing shy of spectacular
through a rarefied atmosphere.

In some far-out way we're
just as close and distant
as Delta Librae,

a binary, stellar companions
orbiting each other, a mutual
centre of gravity,
stabilised by dynamic energy
of our own making,
yet not of our making.

Synergetic starlight are we.

We thrive in the same space,
interchange fire,
infuse love and diverse
modes to admire
one another's relative motion;
think worlds
of our collaborative coronae
never having an inclination
to accept

somewhere and somewhen
this was blue-printed
by universal intelligence.

For an occluded, intersecting
kindred cosmos may
exist with a parallactic view
of me and you:
two similar, dissimilar selves
opting for disparity.

ROUNDS

The girth of grim reality
is obscured by midwinter's
brisk atmosphere
while we wind
through the park paths.

We walk on water where
snowy egrets had waded
in summer; their ivory
downcurves topped
by tiny regal crests,
circumscribed feathery
shadows under
January's receding sun.

Everything spins full circle;
a forward glissade
is guaranteed.

Outstretched wings
afire, positioned
for impermanence,
readying for aviation,
projected beyond brief
inconsequential circumstances;
fleeting configurations for us
to observe in a revolving
continuous blur.

NOCTURNAL NOTES

In an outlying wildwood
the falsetto from a fallen
nightjar fills
my ears with its grousing
    off-centre
to my own darkness.

The bulrushes' susurrus
surrounds me amid
ravelled waterways,
a hazy, hidden island
coiled in on itself,
    captivity.

Responding to the night
bird's dirge, I join in its
grievance, protesting
for all noteless others.

Deliverance unfeasible,
consolation past
perceivable dissent,
overshadowed by
subconscious voices.

They too modulated,
palsied from another
unsettled, unfamiliar grove,
bleak staccato waves
foretelling of another demise:
O fruitless paradise!

COMPLEX COURSES

To designate you
a desired destination;
most superlative,
most noteworthy,
not culling the best words
from a seasoned poet's
lexicon nor uprooting
grey bristled rhymes.

That is unequivocal
for I am well-versed
in the subject of You
and love you beyond
all distractions.

My fixed purpose:
an objective curriculum,
hoping to learn more
from your fundamental
teachings through whatever
vast means are necessary
in attaining
the wisdom of love
on complex courses.

BUT SERIOUSLY, FOLKS

Silently going about my off-
balance business of being
Chaplinesque: Little Tramping
with slapstick, exaggerated
expressions & acrobatic
flexibility, showing the world
the zany spaces
my eccentric mind
occasionally enjoys entering,
on what strange frequencies
it likes to misbehave.

My compass of mind
in need of recalibration
as I sever all ties
to the Elean School,
or at least play down
any connections to it.

Confounding my mind-mender
with knockdown arguments
via quotations from Kierkegaard
and Marx. Should I lecture
the United Nations
with witty discourse
on issues of warfare
and a sure-fire means
of ending it for good?

But seriously, folks,
won't you please forgive me,
I almost forgot
what a masquerader I can be,
excuse this role player:
his clownish accoutrements,
his comical steps.

THE ARTIST PAINTS HIMSELF
INTO A HIGH SOCIETY CORNER

Under an idyllic serene sky,
stippled by perspective shadings,
purely by your youthful,
unseasoned yet sophisticated eye,
matted workhorses pulled plows
furrowing your father's fields,
in a backdrop of marguerites.

Meticulous innateness, attention
given to the minutest detail,
admired and approved by your
sensibility, as apt brushes & knives
stroke their characterisation,
and I notice the finesse, seized
with wonder at your tender passion:
reflective, tranquil elements
of this pastoral scene rendered
with seeming ease on canvas.

But then again, that was rural
life in the Summer of 1969.
Those stolid ranch equines
have long since been put out
to pasture. Your work continues
with acrylics and watercolours,
though aficionados demand more
exorbitant, elaborate salable pieces.

Proudly your pristinely painted
thoroughbreds prance upon elegant,
well-kempt Kentucky bluegrass.
Nobody need distort his face
in contempt while bearing witness
to your virtu that's become wolfish
and gone to commercial canines.

For those more noteworthy
than you have often bitten soft hands
that once fed them; have sold out
for ultimate epicurean flavours
of wine & cheese. Suffice to say,
there's still proof of your then-
uncorrupted compassion
contained in that local studio
with the inadequate lighting.

SHIFTS IN PERCEPTION

After sunset,
in blue dusk we walked
beside the black Thames
mottled with sky sentinels
resembling congealed
coups d'oeil
of Palezoic fish.

This is the weekend
we turn the clocks back,
you said, as your son
ran ahead of us,
showing his new-found
independence.
An inquisitive boy,
tilting his head back
to gaze at the stars,
jubilantly asking, *Can we*
take some home, Mom?
Can we?

Later that night,
lying in bed,
I was better able
to perceive the immensity
that lies between our worlds
and the ages.

ACETICS

Again and again
there are those
who can't help
but look the sun
directly in its fat,
florid face,
defying blindness
to be apprised
of its magnitude.

They catch fire
on canvas with colours
and cross-examine
themselves
using euphemisms,
chisel heroes in stone,
and imitate melic birds.

Roundabout ways
unwind, a slippery sidewinder
leads them onward
through black rains.

Sustained by disdain,
they decline to alter
their perspectives,
revel in seclusion even
as the urban sprawl
opens up to take them in.

ARTISTIC MOVEMENTS

Without the aid of ear,
Beethoven nevertheless
heard dulcetness that sound
judgement scored
from his concerted
inner mechanism
with prodigious fidelity.

The deft artisan
who crafts a comely
cameo needs no tactile
testimonial from her qualified
fingers to grasp for more
precise instruments.

Likewise the versifier
whose fading vision
may keep his focus
toward respite with self-
reliance, looking on
his lines with internal
sight, realising universal
truth: they discompose
not his undaunted spirit,
for they shall be acclaimed
by a tincture of time,
and the poetic community's
commendation.

LIVING IN THE CRAZED AGE OF CELEBRITY CULTURE

When I have returned to dust,
recall me, but not the genuine me;
leave that bashful violet be.
Instead, visit the giddy governess
of Cagliari and let her pie-eyes
look back on our escapades,
my most shelfworn banalities
and grey-whiskered anecdotes.
She'll recount in platitudes
with her own twists on them.

Arouse my drinking buddies
to spew about my pseudo-impressions.
Dig up the groundskeeper
and he'll likely kick up a dust
of how I conversed with him daily.
Let everyone know to what degree
I pretended to enjoy the company
of that charlatan novelist.

But most importantly, tell them
of the over-zealous scarecrow
attendants during Long Beach
retreats with accents as flat as tortillas,
tailored in high-strung fashions,
relating afternoons I compared notes
with Leonard Cohen, John Updike
and S. J. Perelman at the Chelsea.

Speak of my wild hair, garish garb
and ecclectic taste in music;
however, never mention in
Montréal nor in Athens how you
annoyed me once, and today
you make the same rounds.

Yes, when I've indeed departed
and am quite out of my misery,
allow just about anything to be said,
everything that is except the truth.
No one ever got to know the real me.
I was the jester of no-one.
Delinquency gave me daring
on the wrong side of forty
and cowardice in my greener days.

NEXUS

For an instant
you were in full swing,
the vivid sun
at a febrile zenith.

A breath later
you bow in transit
to the inclement moon,
the lethargic gravity.

You make contact,
connect, yet merely momentarily
for regression begins:
    you are waning into radiance,
        a pearl-white orientation
        where even blackness
    flirts with fire.

This too to be only temporary:
    you side-glance,
        ride the indiscernible line
            in passage to the dark side,
                foreglimpse the precise moment
                when you will be
            the centre of consciousness
        at middle arc,
    equally disconnected,
symmetrical.

THE LAND OF LIES

By chance it was a subconscious
urge he had for self-destruction,
nonetheless he searched fields
of fabrications in the land of outlandish
lies for death, referring to it rather
as a pale shade of love.

His steady flow of ideas reached
down, seeped into the roots
of the morning glories. Now, I suspect
nettles foster & lurch above on banks
of an unvisited cenotaph.

Years later, rambunctious little
Billy tucks a sheet into the back
of his shirt, pretends he's Superman
with vague memories of his father
lingering in the back of his mind
as he swings on the oak branches
that Daddy planted before he left.

Sprightly Cindy has backyard
tea parties, plays house and dresses
Barbie dolls with designer-like
fashions spun from her vivid imagination.
Creative kids seem more aware
of space-time than any grown-up
lovers whispering the words:
I do , forever & always.

The tiniest of seeds enshrine broken
flowers, each human utterance
seems to contain a falsehood
for the unvarnished truth lacks lustre.
The daytime's darkness chills me
as the distant moon evacuates
the space for which she holds
absolutely no affection.
Tonight I can think of no single
analogy for her apathy.

METTLE AND PATIENCE

Great tender graces
lie in unbroken sleep
in their flagons.
We had bottled them
like wine to ferment
beyond our blessing's
inauguration.
Long opaque casks
of sweetness
corked watertight.
We had cast them
into an oceanic cavern
where rugged charm
and exacting elegance
of a vermilion
filly of fury
dreamt;
harboured them long
in a condition of lofty
conception,
kept fervency
under control
within the fire's
core. The swagger
of assymetrical ideals
fascinated us through
many trying liturgies.
Our mettle and patience
validated its extraordinary
nocturnal, magical
prowess.

OTHER ROUTES

Time I now call my own,
forgetting current itineries,
turning away
from their rocky
paths for they are
all impasses.

Observe the obstacles
that squarely meet
the quartet of seasons,
feel night's galvanised
iron & reinforced
concrete cavalier
on the skyline.

Return smartly
to familiar stomping
grounds, locate
the smallest
of lodgings & dwell
within miniature
spalls.

Consider other routes
to traverse 'til the darkest
abode of earth
is reached.

Pay a social call
to your heart,
trace lifelines
on your palm
proving superior
to the twisted pathways
of this world,
the sudden tempests
sprung on seven seas.

With optimistic scope
focus on the love
you've envisioned
countless times;
her rainbow essence
butterflying toward
you in the cheerful
sun of June.

Breathe softly now,
allow no head winds
to ruffle the air;
let all be easy,
warm and still.

SKETCHES

A champagne dawn
breaks over bordeaux
shallows, tiny ice floes
clink & smack
into one another,
then conjoin on snow-
bearded banks.

A scarcity of geese
wingover in desolate skeins,
pitching & plunging,
attracting attention
from a clacking trumpeter
swan wedge.

Soft growing shadows
eclipse the marble
memorial column.
A small team of teals
mounts the sky's
suspended riven rays.

A sudden soberness
envelops & comforts me.
I begin sketching
the ruffled river
scene in relative,
citified silence.

Circumscribing charcoal
blotches   beeches
and sycamores.
Scrawl, scribble, scratch---
crosshatching
lead carbonate.

The old courthouse
chimes slice the icy air
stirring echoes congregate
in the corridors
of the heart.

Ghostly memories
glowing from a faraway
summer stumble
through a darkened
threshold undeterred
by the draft
in the wake

of wine and candlewax,
spiritedly finding
a musty garret
of imaginative abstraction
drawn to discover
light & warmth.

INGLENOOK IMAGININGS

In front of the fire, in your
faithful brown study, the Gothic
novel falls from your hand,
and you devise greener valleys
where you delight in easygoing
sunny days or impart a blushing
bodily charm to the rhododendron
as scarlet tanagers in branches
rejoice your rumba in the rain.

Upon populating the garden
with your lovers & children,
you believe in pure paradise.
The real world an interval
monopolised by outsiders,
accepted only by the unromantic
since they are strangers
to these types of tomorrows
while the flower of your life
withers in daydreams.
You live in hopes; they just live.

You assign yourself not a future
but a banishment.
When myriad fires have expired
in the hearth whereby you dream,
and the volumes you've read
are consigned to oblivion,
then you will discover
a perpetual summer's aftereffect:

fields of unending white,
the illusion laden with snow,
you'll turn to look away
from that abandoned land,
but like transgressors
or apparitions reappearing
indistinguisable, prowling
at midnight, will still
map out methods
to enter your domain.

THE FAREWELL (The Rest is Silence)

Was it an Iscariotic kiss
from shameless lips,
one last sanctimonious
touch from a greedy, double-
dealing moneyman who
lost interest that disillusioned
and betrayed you;
knocking the props
from beneath your feet?

For the evening's eastbound
A-train transfers your resolve
to move on as I stand
wordless & tearless
on the platform
waving an angonising farewell.

What was the sensation like
to have the masses
cheering your performances;
how did it feel to be the poster
person for a Bohemian fringe?

With what artistry did you
provide for & against rainy day
conditions; preparing a muddy track
for other future long shots?
How did you ever manage
to lay such groundwork
for additional institutions?

Your iron will won't allow you
to return to that unprincipled
power elite:

     despotic dullards
     and insensitive ingrates
     who thoroughly dowsed
     your desire.

Your swan song has reached
its coda, you have made yourself
easy on that particular score,
and now the rest is silence.

The clattering steel wheels
carry you away as I notice
the 6 o'clock sun reflecting off
the back of the silver tube
matches exactly the shade
of rouge on your cheeks.

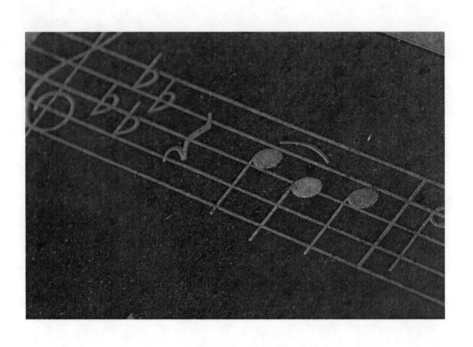

About the Author

Gregory Wm. Gunn has been involved with the arts to varying degrees for over three decades. He is fundamentally self-taught in poetics as well as in the field of music, where he learnt guitar, bass guitar and vocalisation with minimal professional instruction; receiving only limited levels of tutelage.

An avid reader, his major influences include the likes of the following luminous literati: Dylan Thomas, Edgar Allan Poe, Wallace Stevens, Edna St. Vincent Millay, John Steinbeck and Hermann Hesse. This is his third complete collection of verse.

Printed in the United States
105325LV00003B/148-186/P